CHRISTMAS CARDS & GIFTS RECORD BOOK

Room to record ten years of Christmas cards sent and received along with gifts given and received. Undated so that you can use for any years.

This book belongs to

Cover Design by Jean Lee Publishing

CHRISTMAS CARDS & GIFTS FOR THE YEAR:

____

CHRISTMAS CARDS SENT FOR THE YEAR____________

Name:	Address:

CHRISTMAS CARDS SENT FOR THE YEAR____________

Name:	Address:

CHRISTMAS CARDS RECEIVED FOR THE YEAR__________

Name:	Address:

CHRISTMAS CARDS RECEIVED FOR THE YEAR________

Name:	Address:

GIFTS GIVEN FOR THE YEAR__________

Name:	Gift:	Price:

GIFTS GIVEN FOR THE YEAR________

Name:	Gift:	Price:

GIFTS RECEIVED FOR THE YEAR__________

From:	Gift:

GIFTS RECEIVED FOR THE YEAR________

From:	Gift:

CHRISTMAS CARDS & GIFTS FOR THE YEAR:

CHRISTMAS CARDS SENT FOR THE YEAR______________

Name:	Address:

CHRISTMAS CARDS SENT FOR THE YEAR___________

Name:	Address:

CHRISTMAS CARDS RECEIVED FOR THE YEAR__________

Name:	Address:

CHRISTMAS CARDS RECEIVED FOR THE YEAR__________

Name:	Address:

GIFTS GIVEN FOR THE YEAR__________

Name:	Gift:	Price:

GIFTS GIVEN FOR THE YEAR__________

Name:	Gift:	Price:

GIFTS RECEIVED FOR THE YEAR________

From:	Gift:

GIFTS RECEIVED FOR THE YEAR________

From:	Gift:

CHRISTMAS CARDS & GIFTS FOR THE YEAR:

____

CHRISTMAS CARDS SENT FOR THE YEAR____________

Name:	Address:

CHRISTMAS CARDS SENT FOR THE YEAR____________

Name:	Address:

CHRISTMAS CARDS RECEIVED FOR THE YEAR________

Name:	Address:

CHRISTMAS CARDS RECEIVED FOR THE YEAR________

Name:	Address:

GIFTS GIVEN FOR THE YEAR________

Name:	Gift:	Price:

GIFTS GIVEN FOR THE YEAR__________

Name:	Gift:	Price:

GIFTS RECEIVED FOR THE YEAR__________

From:	Gift:

GIFTS RECEIVED FOR THE YEAR__________

From:	Gift:

CHRISTMAS CARDS & GIFTS FOR THE YEAR:

CHRISTMAS CARDS SENT FOR THE YEAR__________

Name:	Address:

CHRISTMAS CARDS SENT FOR THE YEAR___________

Name:	Address:

CHRISTMAS CARDS RECEIVED FOR THE YEAR________

Name:	Address:

CHRISTMAS CARDS RECEIVED FOR THE YEAR________

Name:	Address:

GIFTS GIVEN FOR THE YEAR________

Name:	Gift:	Price:

GIFTS GIVEN FOR THE YEAR__________

Name:	Gift:	Price:

GIFTS RECEIVED FOR THE YEAR________

From:	Gift:

GIFTS RECEIVED FOR THE YEAR________

From:	Gift:

CHRISTMAS CARDS & GIFTS FOR THE YEAR:

____

CHRISTMAS CARDS SENT FOR THE YEAR__________

Name:	Address:

CHRISTMAS CARDS SENT FOR THE YEAR__________

Name:	Address:

CHRISTMAS CARDS RECEIVED FOR THE YEAR__________

Name:	Address:

CHRISTMAS CARDS RECEIVED FOR THE YEAR________

Name:	Address:

GIFTS GIVEN FOR THE YEAR_________

Name:	Gift:	Price:

GIFTS GIVEN FOR THE YEAR________

Name:	Gift:	Price:

GIFTS RECEIVED FOR THE YEAR__________

From:	Gift:

GIFTS RECEIVED FOR THE YEAR__________

From:	Gift:

CHRISTMAS CARDS & GIFTS FOR THE YEAR:

____

CHRISTMAS CARDS SENT FOR THE YEAR__________

Name:	Address:

CHRISTMAS CARDS SENT FOR THE YEAR___________

Name:	Address:

CHRISTMAS CARDS RECEIVED FOR THE YEAR________

Name:	Address:

CHRISTMAS CARDS RECEIVED FOR THE YEAR________

Name:	Address:

GIFTS GIVEN FOR THE YEAR__________

Name:	Gift:	Price:

GIFTS GIVEN FOR THE YEAR________

Name:	Gift:	Price:

GIFTS RECEIVED FOR THE YEAR________

From:	Gift:

GIFTS RECEIVED FOR THE YEAR________

From:	Gift:

CHRISTMAS CARDS & GIFTS FOR THE YEAR:

____

CHRISTMAS CARDS SENT FOR THE YEAR__________

Name:	Address:

CHRISTMAS CARDS SENT FOR THE YEAR___________

Name:	Address:

CHRISTMAS CARDS RECEIVED FOR THE YEAR________

Name:	Address:

CHRISTMAS CARDS RECEIVED FOR THE YEAR________

Name:	Address:

GIFTS GIVEN FOR THE YEAR________

Name:	Gift:	Price:

GIFTS GIVEN FOR THE YEAR__________

Name:	Gift:	Price:

GIFTS RECEIVED FOR THE YEAR________

From:	Gift:

GIFTS RECEIVED FOR THE YEAR________

From:	Gift:

CHRISTMAS CARDS & GIFTS FOR THE YEAR:

____

CHRISTMAS CARDS SENT FOR THE YEAR___________

Name:	Address:

CHRISTMAS CARDS SENT FOR THE YEAR___________

Name:	Address:

CHRISTMAS CARDS RECEIVED FOR THE YEAR_________

Name:	Address:

CHRISTMAS CARDS RECEIVED FOR THE YEAR________

Name:	Address:

GIFTS GIVEN FOR THE YEAR________

Name:	Gift:	Price:

GIFTS GIVEN FOR THE YEAR________

Name:	Gift:	Price:

GIFTS RECEIVED FOR THE YEAR________

From:	Gift:

GIFTS RECEIVED FOR THE YEAR________

From:	Gift:

CHRISTMAS CARDS & GIFTS FOR THE YEAR:

____

CHRISTMAS CARDS SENT FOR THE YEAR____________

Name:	Address:

CHRISTMAS CARDS SENT FOR THE YEAR____________

Name:	Address:

CHRISTMAS CARDS RECEIVED FOR THE YEAR________

Name:	Address:

CHRISTMAS CARDS RECEIVED FOR THE YEAR________

Name:	Address:

GIFTS GIVEN FOR THE YEAR__________

Name:	Gift:	Price:

GIFTS GIVEN FOR THE YEAR__________

Name:	Gift:	Price:

GIFTS RECEIVED FOR THE YEAR__________

From:	Gift:

GIFTS RECEIVED FOR THE YEAR________

From:	Gift:

CHRISTMAS CARDS & GIFTS FOR THE YEAR:

____

CHRISTMAS CARDS SENT FOR THE YEAR____________

Name:	Address:

CHRISTMAS CARDS SENT FOR THE YEAR___________

Name:	Address:

CHRISTMAS CARDS RECEIVED FOR THE YEAR________

Name:	Address:

CHRISTMAS CARDS RECEIVED FOR THE YEAR________

Name:	Address:

GIFTS GIVEN FOR THE YEAR__________

Name:	Gift:	Price:

GIFTS GIVEN FOR THE YEAR__________

Name:	Gift:	Price:

GIFTS RECEIVED FOR THE YEAR________

From:	Gift:

GIFTS RECEIVED FOR THE YEAR________

From:	Gift:

Printed in Great Britain
by Amazon

33705461R00059